# A GUIDE TO

# AMERICAN INDIAN BEADWORK

## OF THE SOUTHWEST

WESTERN NATIONAL PARKS ASSOCIATION
Tucson, Arizona

Published by Western National Parks Association

The net proceeds from WNPA publications support education and research programs in the national parks. To learn more, visit *www.wnpa.org*.

Written by Rose Houk
Edited by Abby Mogollón
Designed by Dawn DeVries Sokol
Photography by George H. H. Huey
Printing by Everbest Printing Company

Cover is a Navajo powwow medallion, artist anonymous.
Title page shows a "cow's head," attributed to a Zuni elder.
Page 5, Navajo folk art, Sheila Antonio; page 6, Navajo beaded basket, Bessie Holiday; page 8, Navajo beaded basket, Bessie Holiday.

Special thanks to Bill and Dollie Beaver, Janet Cantley, Claudia Cellicion, Diane Dittemore, Gregg Leighton, Kent Morrow, Dolly Rich, Daisy Simms, Barry Simpson, Georgiana Simpson, and Isabel Tovar.

Items on pages 12, 21, 23, 25, 27, 29, 31, 35, 37, 39, 43, and 45 courtesy of the Arizona State Museum.

ISBN-10: 1-58369-109-X
ISBN-13: 978-1-58369-109-0

Printed in China

# ❊ CONTENTS ❊

Introduction ............................................. 4

Bags, Purses, and Pouches ......................... 10

Baskets ................................................. 14

Basket Miniatures ................................... 16

Belts, Sashes, Hatbands ............................ 18

Bola Ties .............................................. 20

Bracelets .............................................. 22

Clothing ............................................... 24

Collars ................................................. 26

Cradleboards .......................................... 28

Cradleboard Miniatures ............................. 30

Figurines .............................................. 32

Hair Ornaments ...................................... 34

Moccasins ............................................. 36

Necklaces .............................................. 38

Powwow Clothing .................................... 40

Souvenirs .............................................. 42

Souvenir Pins ......................................... 44

Beading Terms ....................................... 46

# INTRODUCTION

From early times the people of North America made beads of seed, bone, stone, and shell. Eastern tribes traded beads of purple or white shell called wampum, while Indians on the Great Plains dyed porcupine quills and stitched them onto animal skins. And in the Southwest, beads of natural materials are found from far back in time.

Manufactured beads arrived with the first Europeans, who, when they sailed to the New World, carried barrels of glass beads as ballast for their ships. In 1540 Spaniards brought beads into the Southwest; in 1598 the Oñate expedition carried some eighty thousand glass beads into New Mexico as trade items and gifts. Fur traders and missionaries also introduced commercial glass beads into the West, and these beads became a primary medium of exchange with tribes. In the mid-1700s, for example, a mountain man could trade a six-foot string of beads for one beaver pelt.

These glass beads were made on the other side of the world. The Venetian island of Murano was the biggest source, but by the early nineteenth century Czechoslovakia had surpassed Italy as the main exporter of beads. Glass seed beads, named for their size and resemblance to plant seeds, appealed to southwestern Indians for their more uniform shapes and enticing, bright colors.

From the 1860s through the 1880s, with the imposition of reservations on tribes, beads were among the goods allotted by treaties. The relatively sedentary reservation life meant more time for activities such as beading. Local trading posts began to carry an enormous selection of beads and these, along with finished beading pieces, became trade items. Girls learned to bead and create their own designs through craft guilds. Beading was taught to students in boarding schools, to hospital patients, and in more recent times as part of tribal economic development programs.

In the early twentieth century, popular ladies' periodicals brought American Indian beadwork to the greater public, offering "Antique Edwardian Apache" bead loom patterns. As tourists began to arrive in the Southwest, beaders took

advantage of that new market. The revival of powwows and other celebrations after World War II fanned demand. Today, serious collectors bring recognition to some beadworkers, pay prices to match, and have ignited an interest in old beadwork.

## Beads

After the Spanish padres introduced trade and rosary beads, another type of large glass bead, the pony bead (so called because of the way it was transported), gained popularity. Pony beads usually came in black, white, or limited colors. The smaller glass seed beads, however, offered a much larger array of choices in glistening colors, cuts, and textures. Over time, beads got progressively smaller and were used more decoratively and ornately. Today Czech, Italian, French, and Japanese suppliers export an impressive line of beads to the United States—opaque, translucent, hex, gel, and rocaille types among them. Retailers and traders buy beads by the kilo and sell them by the hank or by the pound. Bead sizes are shown by numbers: the larger the number, the smaller the bead. Large pony beads are 8s, for example, while seed beads range from sizes 10 to 22. Sizes 11 to 14 are popular, while a size 16 is almost unworkable for most beaders.

Beaders make very conscious color choices, finding inspiration in the stunning landscapes of their homelands, in tradition and symbolism, and in individual preference and creativity. With the development of a modern "pan-Indian" style of beadwork, it can be tricky to assign strict tribal identity to pieces based on color choices.

Designs can be as simple as a single row of bead edging, or lines of beads along a seam, or as complex as coverage of every square inch of fabric in intricate beading. Color is integral to design, and some beaders skillfully use foreground and background colors to compose designs with contrast and depth. Patterns range from geometrics to florals to pictorials. Sequins, metal buttons, tin cones, fringe, and tassels embellish some pieces, lending dimension, texture, and even sound when a piece is worn in a dance, for instance. Some beadworkers say designs come to them in dreams. When they see the beads, they're inspired and just follow their instincts.

There are two basic beading techniques: beads are stitched with needle and thread or woven in strips on a loom. Originally, beadworkers stitched by punching holes with a bone awl in supple, buttery soft, brain-tanned buckskin, then applied the beads. Beadwork was done not just on buckskin or rawhide but also on a woven wool fabric called baize or on cotton calico. Modern backing materials can be anything from leather and vinyl to chamois, canvas, and velvet. In fact, a single piece of beadwork can incorporate several crafts—such as basketry, jewelry making, and leatherwork.

Animal sinew served as thread in the old days, but now beadworkers use imitation sinew, nylon, or cotton thread.

Beaders often coat the thread with beeswax to keep it from tangling and to make it last longer. Special beading needles are available—long ones for loom work and shorter ones for sewing. Beadworkers employ several different types of stitches and most commonly use the lane or lazy stitch, appliqué or overlay stitch, and peyote or gourd stitch. A bow strung with warp thread served as an early beading loom; today a homemade loom can range from a wooden board with a hair comb at each end for the warp strings to store-bought models made just for beading.

Traditionally, beadwork was done for personal use and was applied to clothing, footwear, accessories, jewelry, and cradleboards. As a tourist market grew in the Southwest, beaders adapted by making what would sell. Regalia or powwow outfits and paraphernalia opened yet another niche. Today the inventory of beaded pieces is dizzying, from unique high-end collector pieces to less expensive, smaller articles such as barrettes, belt buckles, key chains, and earrings.

Collectors can find beadwork throughout the Southwest. As with many other native arts and crafts, traders have heavily influenced forms, colors, and patterns. If you want to know more about beadwork and beaders, ask a trader or ask a beader. All are eager to share their enthusiasm for this fascinating, irre-sistible art. The best way to acquire an authentic piece is to buy directly from the artist or from a reputable museum or dealer.

# Bags, Purses, and Pouches

BEADED BAGS AND POUCHES have long been used by native people. They came in a variety of sizes and shapes—square, rectangular, and round—and served a host of functions. There were medicine bags, tobacco pouches, pipe bags, awl cases, knife sheaths, mirror pouches, bags to hold fire-making equipment, and even purses to carry ration tickets once Indians were forced to live on reservations. And in a bag of her own making, a beadworker could carry all the necessary materials for this most portable of crafts.

Bags that combined both loom and stitched beading were distinct to Ute people. Historically, Utes traded their beaded bags along with hides, robes, and horses for Navajo blankets, silver, and crops. This trade stimulated the spread of ideas among beaders of different tribes.

Beaded bags are still being made and used today, though they may serve slightly different functions.

Anonymous, *Ute, 1980*

Historic, *Mescalero Apache, circa 1880s*

John Willie, *Navajo, 2006*

# BASKETS

BASKETS ARE AN EXCELLENT example of ongoing innovation in beading. Beaders display remarkable skills in use of intricate patterns and colors. The genesis of this form may be traced back to Ute-Paiute beader Alice Lang, who was encouraged by the late Robert Leighton, owner of Notah Dineh Trading Company in Cortez, Colorado. Lang pursued this work and created some huge baskets containing nearly six hundred thousand individual beads. Betty Hathale and family, Navajos from Red Mesa, have also created beautiful pieces, often using woven O'odham baskets wrapped in cotton or other cloth as the foundation.

Betty Hathale, *Navajo, circa 1980*

# BASKET MINIATURES

THE BLANDING, UTAH, AREA boasts a wealth of talented artists who have raised beaded basketry to exquisite levels. Shirley Kills-In-Sight covers baskets of yucca and sweetgrass with leather before beading them. She starts at the bottom of the basket, stitching beads of red, yellow, white, green, blue, and orange—what she calls "fire," "earth," and "rainbow" colors. The tiny beads and ornate designs are transformed into breathtaking baskets, some of them in miniature form.

Shirley says, "I do prayer when I do my beadwork. I pray and say . . . thank you for the colors and the designs you gave me."

Shirley Kills-In-Sight, *Navajo, 2005*

# BELTS, SASHES, HATBANDS

BEADED BELTS, SASHES, ARMBANDS, hatbands, choker
necklaces, and blanket strips are more often created with
a loom rather than by stitching. They are made by stringing
warp threads on a loom wide enough and long enough to
accommodate the finished piece. Then beads carried on a
needle and thread are woven at right angles to the warp to
create the design, often repeated geometrics or florals.

After World War II, Bill Richardson of Richardson's
Trading Company in Gallup, New Mexico, got Czech beads
from New York and employed a hundred Navajo beaders,
working at their homes, to bead loomed strips for which they
were paid by the inch. Women sewed those strips onto leather
belts, which were then sold all over the country. When the
Japanese began to make similar but much cheaper versions in
the early 1960s, Richardson's enterprise ended, but belts are
still very much part of the repertoire of beaders today.

Anonymous, *Ute sash, circa 1970s*

# BOLA TIES

ONE DICTIONARY DEFINES a bola tie as "a necktie consisting of a piece of cord fastened with an ornamental bar or clasp." The official neckwear of both Arizona and New Mexico, the bola tie rules as the epitome of traditional western dress.

Beaders haven't missed out on the opportunity to incorporate their medium into this quintessential fashion statement. Beaded bolas display various colors and designs, sometimes with belt buckles to match. Both the cord and the clasp may be beaded, or clasps may be made of silver or turquoise.

Blackie family, *Navajo, circa 1970s*

# BRACELETS

BEADED BRACELETS—along with other smaller jewelry and accessory pieces such as earrings, belt buckles, and barrettes—are popular items made for sale. Navajo beaders have been especially prolific and successful at making and selling bracelets.

Beads hold deep symbolism for Navajos. Their six sacred mountains are said to be dressed with beads of sacred colors, and White Bead (Shell) Woman is a central figure in their cosmology. One historian says the Navajo were creating sewn beadwork as early as the 1700s. By the early twentieth century they were learning the craft at boarding schools and producing work for sale at trading posts.

Even today, Navajo beaders say their land most inspires their choice of colors and designs. When scholar Ellen Moore talked with many of these beadworkers, she found that the trio of natural phenomena mentioned most often as inspiration included fire, rainbows, and sunsets.

Magoosh family, *Mescalero Apache, 1994*

# Clothing

CLOTHES PROVIDE ANOTHER CANVAS upon which beaders can display their art. The earliest beaded clothing was made of buckskin, and a woman's skill at tanning deer or other hides was admired as much as her beadwork. After contact with Europeans, women turned to adorning commercial cloth—wool, cotton, or velveteen—with beads.

Men's shirts, jackets, vests, and leggings were beaded down the arms, across the shoulders, and over breastplates. To complete their outfits, Ute men wrapped their long braids with beads, wore beaded chokers, and robed themselves in blankets with beaded strips. Western Apache and Navajo men also wore hide "warrior" shirts embellished with beads.

Traditionally, Apache women might apply a simple band of blue and white beads to a yoke or seam. Ute women wore beaded dresses, either elaborate or adorned with simple lane-stitched beads. Ute beadwork often showed influences from the Lakota and other Plains beaders, as well as from their close neighbors, the Jicarilla Apache.

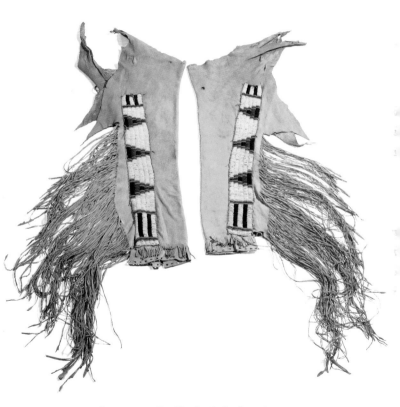

Anonymous, *Jicarilla Apache leggings, circa 1880s*

# COLLARS

MOHAVE, QUECHAN, AND COCOPAH beaders of the lower Colorado River area have manufactured beaded collars for more than a century. The word "collar" hardly does justice to these complex pieces. Glass seed beads are stitched in a netting technique, starting at the neck and widening out to a full circle, then finishing with straight or looped bead fringe. The small beads and artistic skill create a mesh effect almost like fine crocheted lacework.

The collar attaches at the neck and lies over the shoulders and chest. Traditional colors for the collars include blue and white or red, black, and white; however, decidedly nontraditional colors exist too—orange and black for instance. Specific elements of the geometric designs have been identified as symbols of turtle shells and the banks of the river where these tribes live. Today, women wear beaded collars as part of traditional dress.

Western Apache and Paiute beaders, among others, also make beaded collars.

*Anonymous, Quechan, circa 1880s*

# CRADLEBOARDS

NOT SURPRISINGLY, NATIVE beadworkers devote extra attention to decorating the cradleboards in which they carry their infants. Common to most cradleboards is a flat back piece with a rounded top, a shade over the child's face, and a pouch with ties to hold the baby snugly against the board. Yet each tribe employs unique construction details and beading styles that identify a cradleboard as its own.

Apaches frequently use yucca stalks for the face shade, paint the board yellow or cover it with yellow cloth, then apply a row or two of beads around the edge of the hood and down the center front. Circles are common design elements. Utes attach willow shoots for the sunshade, wood boards or vertical willow slats for the back, and fringed buckskin wrapping. They place an evenly spaced pattern of beads, either stitched or woven, on a wide band along the curved top of the backboard, on the hood, and on the front pouch.

On some cradleboards, a beaded awl case or umbilical cord pouch is attached.

Wayne and Carrie Marsh, *Ute, 2005*

# CRADLEBOARD MINIATURES

BEADERS SHOW A PLAYFUL yet practical side when they create delightful miniature pieces. These are made mostly for toys, gifts, or sale items. Charming cradleboards, baskets, moccasins, and cloth dolls are often exact replicas, faithful in every detail to the full-sized versions.

Anonymous, *Mescalero Apache, circa 1910*

# FIGURINES

THE ZUNI OF WESTERN New Mexico are well known for their beaded figurines. Fashioned in rich colors and with realistic detail, the pieces range from horses with riders to "Comanche" figures, Zuni maidens complete with water jars on their heads, and amazing dance plaza scenes. Almost anything that inspires the artist can be translated into a beaded sculpture.

The craft may have gotten started at Zuni in the 1920s at the urging of trader C. G. Wallace for the tourist market. Now whole families participate in making figurines.

At first, foundations consisted of cloth, sticks, and even watermelon seeds! Now the base is often carved of wood then covered with cloth, and the beads stitched on one at a time. The figures range from an inch or two up to twelve inches tall. Size determines how long each piece takes to complete.

Claudia Cellicion, *Zuni, circa 2000s*

# Hair Ornaments

The Apache are known for a unique hourglass-shaped hair ornament of beads stitched onto a hide or cloth backing. Traditionally, young women wear the ornaments through the time they are married and become pregnant with their first child. This wearable art was still being made and sold at trading posts on Apache reservations in recent years.

Beaders use hair ornaments for both traditional and playful expressions of life and culture.

Doris Gilbert, *San Carlos Apache, 1996*

# MOCCASINS

FOOTWEAR HAS LONG been the foremost item on which southwestern beadworkers show off their craft. Moccasins of rawhide and buckskin sport a variety of beading designs. Floral and medallion motifs trim the instep and accentuate the toes of moccasins, or a few bands of beads outline the edges or ankle section.

As with cradleboards, moccasin construction styles are often clues to the affiliation of the makers. Utes fashioned two-piece moccasins with tough rawhide soles and soft, brain-tanned hide uppers. Apaches made buckskin moccasins that reached to the knee, mid-calf, or ankle with distinct turned up "toe tabs" on the tips—maybe to ward off rocks and cactus spines, or perhaps just as a fashion statement. Sparsely beaded, they often bore a braided rope-effect pattern in two colors.

The beaded moccasin tradition has carried over to modern footwear, so that now you may spy beading even on someone's tennis shoes!

Shima, *Chiricachua Apache, 1912*

# NECKLACES

BEADED T-SHAPED necklaces reportedly are unique to the Western Apache. Apache girls wear T-shaped necklaces as part of their elaborate dresses for their puberty ceremonies.

Before 1900 beaders used a peyote stitch to form the striking geometric patterns. Since that time, the necklaces have most often been woven on looms.

Beaders sew a horizontal band and a vertical band together to form the "T" shape. Triangles, hexagons, and diamonds are the norm, but occasionally a beader will incorporate an eagle motif or even *gaan* figures, representations of Apache spiritual beings. Common necklace colors are yellow and white, along with red, blue, and green. Some beaders make T-shaped necklaces to be sold.

Anonymous, *Western Apache, circa 1890s*

# Powwow Clothing

WHEN A LARGE GROUP of dancers files out onto the floor for the grand entry at a powwow, the scene is a mesmerizing whirl of sights and sounds—insistent drumbeats; whoops and cries as the dancers dip and sway; and flashes of feathers, fringes, mirrors, tinklers, and of course beadwork. Many dancers, it seems, are beaded from head to foot—crowns, hairpieces, dresses, shirts, belts, leggings, and moccasins—in an incredible display of sparkling colors.

With American Indians coming from all over the country to participate in these intertribal get-togethers, demand for powwow clothing and paraphernalia is huge. A beader may make the pieces for a relative or friend. Dancers also have access to beadwork through traders, artists who specialize in powwow pieces, and beadworkers who advertise on the Internet.

Anonymous, *Ute hair ornaments, circa 1990s*

# Souvenirs

Southwestern beaders have always demonstrated a great capacity for creative adaptation, especially in satisfying the market's demand for souvenir and curio pieces. Popular in the 1930s, beaded rabbit feet fed the tourist trade of the time. Today almost anything is fair game for beading—you will find beaded jars, along with beaded bottle caps, key chains, eyeglass holders, and even toothbrush cases, ice buckets, and dog collars.

Maryann Burdette, *San Carlos Apache beaded jar, 1959*

# SOUVENIR PINS

BEADED FORMS CAN be whimsical and unexpected, limited only by the artist's imagination. The Cocopah are influenced by the animals that live in their desert home along the lower Colorado River, and they render those creatures in delightful beaded pins for sale as souvenirs.

Betty Thomas, *Cocopah, 1994*

# Beading Terms

Appliqué stitch: Also called running or overlaid stitch, appliqué uses two threads: one carrying the beads and a second to tack down the beads at intervals. This stitch fills in the space of a curved design or can be worked on a flat piece to create long parallel lines of solid beadwork without visible rows or ridges.

Greasy yellows: Older glass beads named for their subtle buttery yellow color. Their use can indicate a beading piece is old, but this method of identification is not foolproof because older beads can be reused or may have come from long-held stock in a warehouse.

Hex beads: Glass beads with faceted surfaces. Beaders like them for that reason, but the beads' sharp edges can cut the thread, a definite disadvantage.

Lane stitch: One of the most common stitches found in beadwork. Lane stitch is also called lazy stitch because six or so beads are strung on the thread at one time, laid in, and stitched down, thus making the work go faster than it would stitching one bead at a time. The artist creates a band of beadwork by sewing each row down beside its neighbor.

PEYOTE STITCH: Also known as gourd stitch, this technique results in a diagonal pattern. A first row of beads is laid down, each bead in the second row is centered between two beads on the first row, and then beads on the third row follow the first row. The effect is much like laying down bricks. Most desirable are very small beads of uniform size.

PONY BEADS: Early glass beads in size 8 or larger, so named because they were brought to the West on the backs of horses or mules beginning around 1820. They were also called pound beads for the rate of exchange—one pound of the beads was worth a finished buffalo robe or a good horse.

SEED BEADS: Glass beads in a flattened, globular shape that range from about $\frac{1}{16}$ to $\frac{1}{8}$ inch in diameter. These are the beads most commonly used today, made in several European countries and Japan, and imported and supplied to retailers and traders in the Southwest.

SINEW: A mammal tendon is cleaned and dried then moistened as sewing thread. Early beaders used sinew, which has been largely replaced today with other materials.

WHITE HEARTS: Older glass beads with a white core and red outer layer. They are still being made today but are expensive.

ALSO FROM
WESTERN NATIONAL PARKS ASSOCIATION

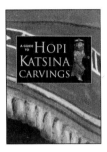

A Guide to Hopi Katsina Carvings
By Rose Houk
ISBN 1-58639-038-7

A Guide to Pueblo Pottery
By Susan Lamb
ISBN 1-877856-62-2

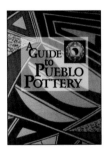

A Guide to Zuni Fetishes
and Carvings
By Susan Lamb
ISBN 1-58369-028-X

*See your bookseller or visit our online bookstore at www.wnpa.org*